DESIGNING WORKSHEETS

PRESENTATION TECHNIQUES FOR TEXTILE STUDENTS

Jan Messent

Contents

Introduction	Page	3
Tools and Materials		4
Preparation of Textile Samples		6
Single Window Mount		8
Double Window Mount		11
Shaped Window Mount		12
Alternative Frame Mounts		14
Single Fabric Mount		15
The Worksheet		16
Choosing the Format		20
Mounts with Spines		22
Multiple Arrangements		23
Preparation of Fabric and Threads		28
Annotations and Lettering		30
Decorating the Worksheet		33
Fixing the Worksheet to the Display Board		35
Notes, Extra Samples and Reference Material		36
Portfolio for A2 Papers		38
Worksheet Corner-protectors		40

INTRODUCTION

It is now accepted practice for textile students to display their work, in design and technique, at the end of the term or course, and to present other course work in such a way that tutors and assessors can form an impression of their standard easily and in a methodical manner. Whether in school or college, every student, child or adult, produces a mountain of material for reference, for inspiration, for experiment and technical exercise, some of which is more relevant to a theme than other parts. To make sure that the right people see the right bits, it is important that they should be presented in the best possible way and displayed so that themes and subjects are in order, correlated attractively and with some purpose. The care shown at this stage goes a long way towards the final impression and reflects the attitude and commitment of the student to the course work.

There are other reasons for taking care over presentation. Among those who attend end-of-course and assessment exhibitions are potential clients and employers. For any textile artist who wishes to work to commission it is essential to show that the working methods from design to completion have been fully thought through, problems understood and coped with and options given in a way which the client can see and understand. Work-sheets, beautifully arranged and annotated in a professional way can make all the difference between acceptance and rejection; it will not make a poor design good, but it will certainly help to raise an ordinary design onto a different level of interest.

Selection for exhibitions often takes place by jurors who understand how to appreciate well-presented work, and colour coordinated design work-sheets alongside a finished project arouse much interest and admiration from both selection committee and visitors to an exhibition. Not only does this look good, but size-related pieces are certainly easier to handle and transport, both for the artist and the organisers, especially when they all fit neatly into a custom-made portfolio. Most impressive! Those who have ever had to take their display work on their travels will appreciate the sense of this.

In all this talk of students, it is not forgotten that teachers and tutors rely on their displays of samples for day-to-day teaching and the example of well-presented pieces must leave an impression on the minds of students as something to be emulated. The tutor must also be able to suggest other methods of display, loose-leaf books, folios, stand-up work-sheets and multiple presentations, and to demonstrate the finishing touches of annotations and coordinating design/decoration which is linked to the source of inspiration. As time is always at a premium, it is hoped that this collection of ideas and information will meet with their approval and that it will help to set new standards of presentation to a wider range of textile students.

Tools and Materials

Important: keep your tools in a safe place, keep them clean and use them only for your craft work.

1. A steel rule is not only for measuring but also for guiding the craft-knife when cutting. Buy the longest one you can afford.

2. Plastic transparent ruler, 12"/30cms long; needed for accurate measuring. Don't use it in place of a steel rule because this accidently cuts notches out of the edge which makes it useless for ruling straight lines.

A tee-square is useful, but not essential. A set-square is useful for checking right-angled corners.

3. Mounting card: this is available in different thicknesses, 4-sheet being thin and bendy, 6-sheet being thicker and good for window-mounting, 8-sheet being extra thick and much less bendy. Card is also obtainable in a huge variety of colours and several different surface-textures, and each sheet measures approximately 32" x 21" /' 81.5 x 53.5 cms. This size is not easy to take by public transport in a flimsy bag! Don't try to cut this type of card with scissors (you will ruin your scissors, the card and your fingers) but always use a very sharp craft-knife. Avoid handling the absorbent coloured surface of the card as finger-marks show.

4. Craft-knife: there is a huge variety to choose from; some have extra blades in the handle, some have retractable blades for safety, and some are too light for cutting card of the thickness we use for mounting. Choose a sturdy but not too heavy model preferably with break-off blades like the one shown here, and ensure that the blade is razor-sharp before use on every occasion.

5. Scissors: for cutting fabric, paper and tapes. Must be sharp.

6. Pencil: HB or H: keep it sharp at all times.

7. Rubber: large soft variety. Keep it clean by scrubbing it in soapy water with a nail-brush.

8. Compass: useful for drawing curves, or whenever you require a circular window.

9. Cutting mat: vital if you are to avoid damaging the table or floor! This is a specially made bendy mat , dark green with white guide-lines, which is placed under the card before cutting begins. All cuts on it "heal" immediately so, with care, it will last for ever. Available at good art/craft supplies: expensive, but worth it. Alternatively, use several thicknesses of clean, smooth cardboard; anything too hard will ruin your knife-blade.

10. Glue: use either the white latex type or clear. In any case it must be strong and clean and preferably have a brush inside the lid. "Stick adhesives" are not strong enough for mounting purposes. Double-sided adhesive strip (on a roll) is very useful for holding fine bits together.

11. Tapes: plastic parcel tape is useful for finishing off the back of work-sheets where it will not be seen. Masking tape has its uses but is not really strong enough to hold heavy card pieces. Linen carpet tape is used for joining card pieces where a fold-over display is required, and as this will be seen from the right side, it must be the same colour as the card being used. If this is a problem, it is perfectly possible to make your own using strips of heavy- duty (pelmet weight) non-woven interfacing (English Vilene) and paint it to match your card. The tape should be 2"/5cms wide. Carpet tape is obtainable from D.I.Y. stores and ironmogers.

12. Strong brown paper: this is used for covering over the back of the card mount after all the pieces have been glued down. It not only makes the display neat but also protects it during constant handling.

13. Sewing cottons, heavy button thread and needles may be necessary on different fabric mounts, but not for a simple card mount.

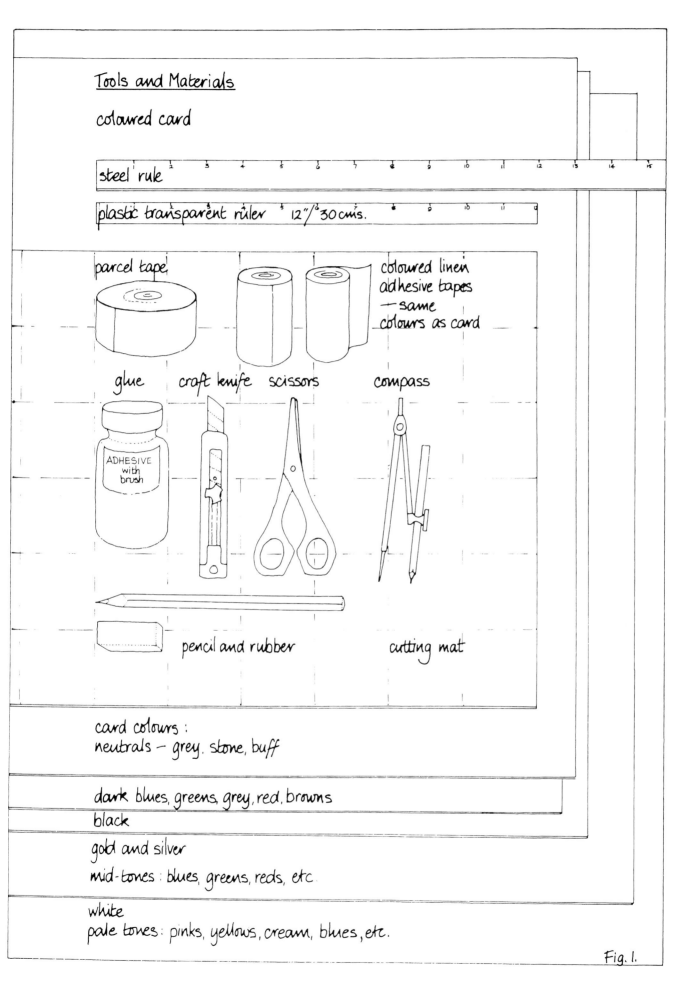

Tools and Materials

coloured card

steel rule

plastic transparent ruler   12″/30 cms.

parcel tape

coloured linen
adhesive tapes
— same
colours as card

glue   craft knife   scissors   compass

ADHESIVE
with
brush

pencil and rubber   cutting mat

card colours :
neutrals — grey, stone, buff

dark blues, greens, grey, red, browns

black

gold and silver

mid-tones : blues, greens, reds, etc.

white
pale tones : pinks, yellows, cream, blues, etc.

Fig. 1.

Preparation of Textile Samples

Textile samples can usually be blocked gently under a damp cloth and a hot iron. Some pieces, especially knitting and crochet may need to be pinned down first to bring them back to their correct shape but they should not take the full weight of the iron. Holding the iron over a damp cloth will usually be enough, thus avoiding the risk of flattening the texture. Velvets are never ironed but held over steam and moved backwards and forwards under tension.

Very fragile fabrics may need to be pre-mounted on a backing of fine non-woven iterfacing (iron-on interfacing is useful for this) before they can be placed under a window- mount.

Trim all ends by darning-in and/or cutting off.

Only the barest amount of surplus fabric should be trimmed off; you will need at least an inch (2.5cms) beyond the size of the window through which it appears. Quilted pieces may need to be tacked or machined all round (outside the window frame) to keep the layers together, otherwise only the top fabric will be stuck to the window and the rest will flap about.

No staples, pins or unwanted stitches should show anywhere once the sample has been mounted. Holes, rust-marks, etc. should all be hidden from view and the glue must never be allowed to seep inside the framed area. It is wise to test it on a piece of fabric to see how it behaves, as some glues discolour fabric and paper quite badly in time.

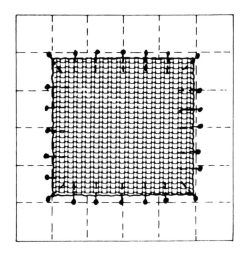

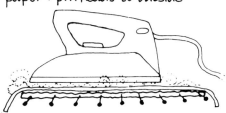

Fig. 2
Sample blocked out on squared paper : pin heads to outside

Steam iron held over damp cloth without resting on top. No pressure required

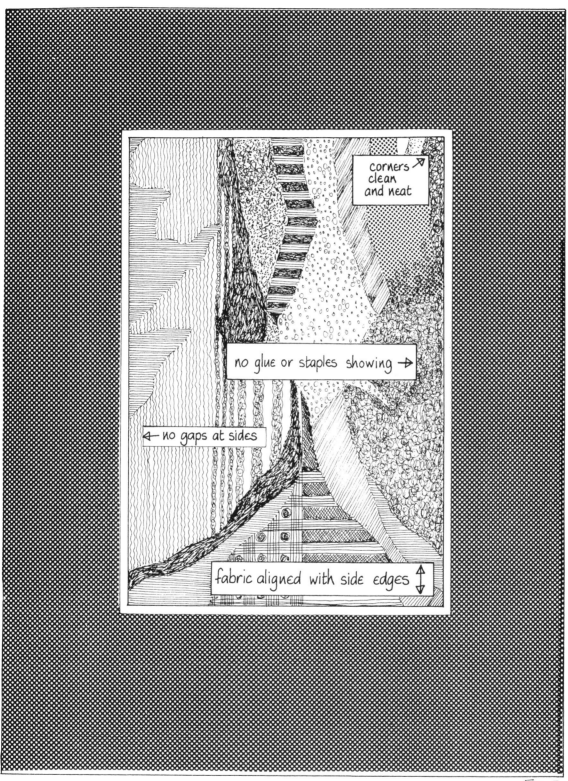

Fig. 3

Single Window Mount

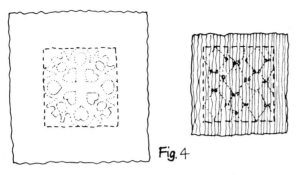

Fig. 4

1. Decide on the exact area of the design to be seen on the right side bearing in mind that, if it is an embroidery, you may wish some of the background fabric to show round the edges of the design. If it is a piece of knitting, crochet or weaving, or something with untidy edges, you may prefer to move the frame in to exclude these parts (Fig. 4). Measure exactly how big the window needs to be and write

mount too large   Fig. 5

mount too small

mount in proportion

this down, e.g. $6\frac{1}{2}$" x $6\frac{1}{2}$"/16.5 x 16.5cms . See also Fig. 9 .

Important: do not cut the fabric to this size.

Some extra fabric will be needed beyond this measurement.

2. Decide on the colour of the card mount. Choose a colour which sets off your work, not necessarily a contrast: one which picks up the main colours often looks best. Neutrals also look good with most colours.

3. Decide on the outside measurements of the card frame. This should not be so large that it swamps the textile nor should it be so narrow that its effect is lost. The proportion is important (Fig. 5).

How to decide: lay the sample down onto the corner of the coloured card so that a wide edge shows all round. Rearrange it until you feel that you have the right amount of frame on two sides then cover up the rest of the surplus card to see how it looks (Fig. 6). Make all four borders the same depth, or make the bottom border slightly deeper than the other three.

4. When you have decided on a satisfactory size and shape for your frame, take accurate measurements of the outer dimensions and write them down. To make things simpler, it helps to take these measurements to the nearest inch or centimetre.

Now you have the inner and outer measurements of the frame.

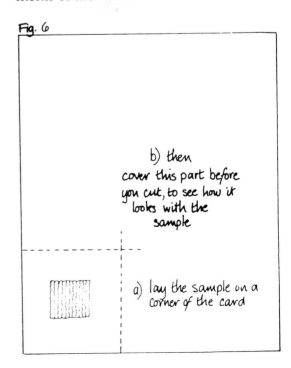

Fig. 6

b) then cover this part before you cut, to see how it looks with the sample

a) lay the sample on a corner of the card

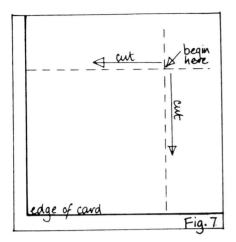

Fig. 7

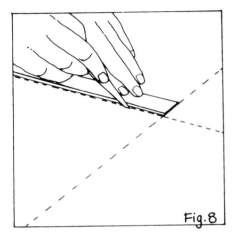

Fig. 8

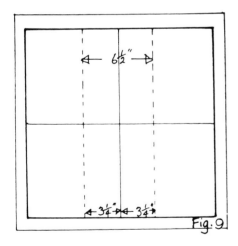

Fig. 9

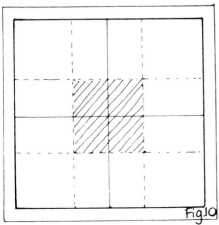

Fig. 10

5. Put the textile piece safely on one side and turn the card over, white side uppermost. All measurements and cutting now take place on the reverse side. Handle the coloured side as little as possible to keep it clean.

6. Working from *one corner* of the card, (i.e. two sides of the frame already cut) measure and draw accurately the outer measurements of the frame. You will only need two pencil lines for this.

7. Place this corner of the card over the cutting mat and lay the steel ruler along one pencil line, vertically. Place the knife-point in the corner where the two pencil lines meet (Fig.7) and draw the blade *gently* down the side of the ruler in one continuous movement (Fig. 8).

8. Keeping the ruler in the same place as before, take a second deeper cut, pulling the knife towards you. This should cut right through the card.

9. Turn the card round so that the second pencil line is now vertical and check that the mat is in place. Lay the steel ruler along this line, exactly, place the knife-blade in the corner again and score down the line gently as before. Now take a second cut right through. The shape should now be free of the larger piece.

10. Still working on the reverse side, find the exact centre of each side and mark it. Now connect these marks from side to side, using a pencil and ruler.

11. To centre the window, divide one side measurement, taken at the first step, in half and adjust it equally on either side of the central vertical line at top and bottom. Connect these lines as shown (Fig. 9).

12. Now take the second side measurement, divide it in half and adjust it equally on either side of the central horizontal line. Connect the lines as before. The area in the centre where these two sets of lines cross is the shape of your window, and this is the area to be cut out (Fig. 10).

9

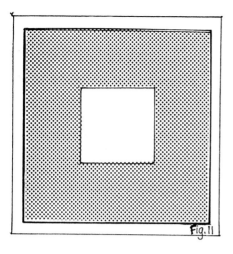

Fig. 11

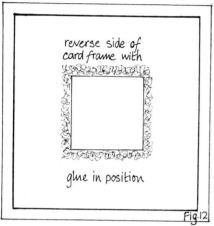

reverse side of
card frame with

glue in position

Fig. 12

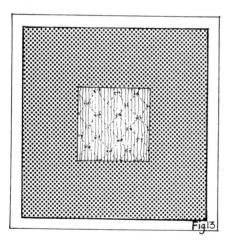

Fig. 13

back of
sample
glued to
frame

back covering-paper to be
glued or taped on dotted lines

Fig. 14

13. Using the mat, steel ruler and knife as before, ALWAYS placing the knife-blade into the corner of the shape and pulling towards you, gently score down the line, then cut right through on the second move. Turn the card round each time so that you are pulling the knife towards you on every cut. Gently push the loose card away from the centre (Fig. 11).

14. On the reverse side, place a line of glue all round the window area of the card (Fig. 12).

15. Place the textile piece flat on the table, hold the card frame, right side up, over the piece and position it carefully before letting it rest fully on top. Press down gently, turn the two pieces over (together) and check that the back is straight and free of wrinkles. Ease the fabric outwards from the centre of the window to stretch it slightly as it dries, turn it to the front again and press again under a piece of clean paper. Any adjustments must be made before the glue dries, so check that the grain of the fabric is straight, that no gaps show, no wrinkles and no bits of extra fibres.

Note: if the textile is extra strong and difficult, it may be necessary to use bulldog clips to hold it in position until the glue dries, but pad the front surface first to prevent the clips making ridges (Fig. 13).

16. To cover the back completely, a piece of brown (parcel) paper should be cut to measurements slightly smaller than the card mount. This is then fixed down all round the edges with parcel or masking tape. Label the mount with your name, address, etc., in one corner, include details of the sample and the date (Fig. 14).

This single mount may, in this condition, be given a wooden frame of the appropriate size, width and colour, but this is not generally necessary for course work.

Double Window Mount

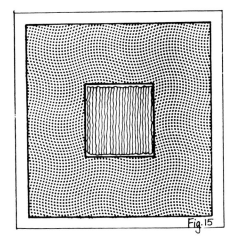

Fig. 15

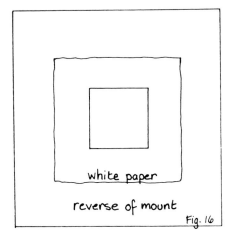

white paper

reverse of mount

Fig. 16

Fig. 17

It sometimes happens that you wish to standardise the size of your mounts and their windows for the sake of unity but discover that some of the pieces are just too small (Fig. 15). In this case, it is perfectly possible to extend their dimensions by making a false frame inside the larger one. Sometimes this actually improves the appearance of the sample, even when it *does* fit'.

For this extra frame, choose a firm heavy-type paper or fine card; ordinary paper will tear in time. Choose white, or a different tone of the mounting-card colour, or gold, silver, any neutral or perhaps black.

Cut the inner frame smaller than the outer one (Fig. 16) with a window just big enough to cover the edges of the sample. Check that this is correct and that an equal amount of the *inside* frame shows inside the larger window of the outer frame. As shown in Fig. 12, place glue on the edges of the outer frame window and place this over the inner frame so that the latter shows just inside, as planned.

Now glue again on the reverse side of the inner frame and place the two frames together over the sample from the right side. Position this carefully before you press down (Fig. 17). Adjust the sample as before, and cover the back.

Shaped Window Mounts

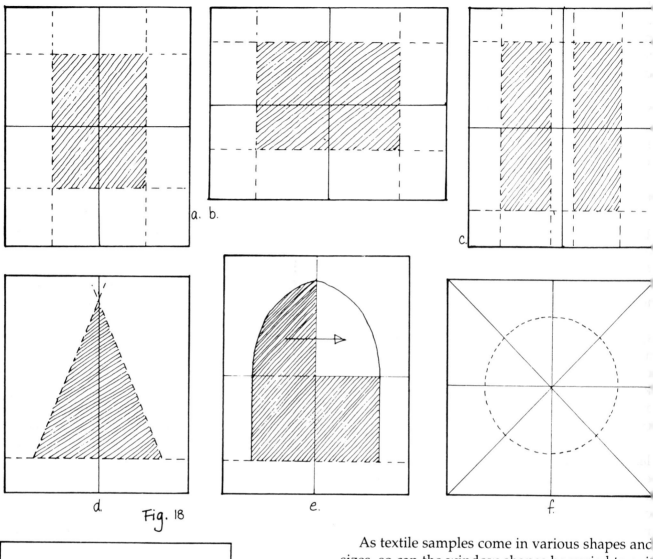

a. b.

c.

d. Fig. 18

e.

f.

Fig. 19

As textile samples come in various shapes and sizes, so can the window shapes be varied to suit them (Fig. 18).

To discover which is the best shape of frame for a sample, first cut a piece of paper, white, brown or coloured, to the required size of the frame (outer dimensions) then cut out a frame which you feel may be appropriate, roughly, with scissors. This may be oblong, square, triangular, circular or oval. An assortment of oblong frames can be created by using two L-shaped pieces of paper or card (Fig. 19). Move these closer or apart over the sample to establish the dimensions of the window.

All this preliminary work can be done quite roughly with scissors, and will help you to make a decision before you begin the final measuring and cutting stage. BUT whatever shape you decide upon, remember that this must not *compete* for interest with the samples themselves, but enhance and complement them.

The oblong mount (Fig.18a and b) is made in the

same way as the single flat mount of square format, but notice that, in these illustrations, the borders at the bottom edges are greater than the ones at the top. They are centred in exactly the same way as before. The dotted lines indicate pencil guide lines.

The oblong two-window mount (Fig. 18c) is useful for long narrow samples where these are not quite important enough to have a mount to themselves. The frame width should be equal at the sides, but be sure that the central part of the frame is wide enough to conceal the join between the two samples.

A triangular window (Fig. l8d) looks best on a square card unless it is long and narrow: an equilateral triangle like this, as with all others, must be centrally aligned and the lower border of the frame should be equal to, or wider than the frame above the top point and the two side edges.

The arched frame (Fig. l8e) also has its uses, especially for samples related to architecture or church work. To make the curves exactly the same on both sides, make a template of one side, cut it out like a paper pattern, then turn it over and draw round it for the other side. Use the central line to guide you when positioning.

The circular frame (Fig. l8f) needs a more complex preparation and the following methods may help but, BE WARNED, cutting a circle is not as easy as cutting a straight-sided figure, it requires accurate measuring, a steady hand, a very sharp knife and patience!

a. As before, measure the card on the reverse side to find the exact centre point and draw lines across to aid positioning.

b. If your compass is not large enough to use, try out various ceramics over your sample to see which fits best, cups, saucers, plates of all dimensions. As you will not be able to tell where the exact centre of the plate lies, measure from the edges of the plate to the edges of the card instead, and when all four measurements are equal, (measured along the four guide lines) you will know that the circle is correctly centred. Now you can draw round the plate.

c. For smaller circles, use a compass by placing the point in the centre of the textile and the pencil point onto the outer edges of the part you wish to be seen. This is the radius of the circle.

d. Keeping the compass point and pencil at the same angle, replace the point in the centre of the card where the two lines cross. Push the point into the card very lightly and move the pencil round until the circle is complete. Be careful not to alter

the angle of the compass while you do this.

e. Before you begin cutting, check again on the size by placing your sample on the circle to make sure that it is large enough. Once the circle is cut, you cannot make it smaller. Make sure that the pencil line is completely continuous, without breaks anywhere: you need all the help you can get once you begin cutting.

f. To cut circles and other curved shapes, read the following hints first. Work on a firm, flat surface cleared of everything except your card, cutting mat and knife. This is to allow you to manoeuvre the card round smoothly as you cut without it catching on anything. Give yourself plenty of room. Never cut right through the card on your first cut, always score it lightly first - just feel your way round with the blade point. Keep strictly to the line and move *very slowly* pulling the hand and arm towards you smoothly. Use a new knife blade and hold the card very firmly to avoid it swinging under the knife as you press down and pull.

When you have scored all round, go round again using more pressure, keeping the knife-blade in the groove but only making tiny moves along the line, moving the card round with your free hand as you go. After the second cut, check the right side to see whether you are through (don't try to push it out too soon) and, if not, take another cut all round in the same groove, with more pressure. Do not be tempted to speed up! On the final cut, the centre should drop out cleanly.

g. The method of assembling the sample and window is the same as for the other shapes. If you should need to trim the edges of the circle, lay the mount down onto the cutting mat and trim from the reverse side with the point of the blade. An emery board is useful to eliminate tiny raggy bits, but be gentle!

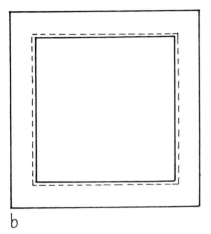

Fig. 20

a

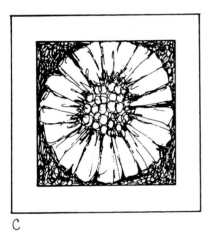

b

c

Alternative Frame Mounts

There are times when a sample is too fragile or too small to mount inside a window (Fig. 20a). In this case, mark out the area on the worksheet without cutting it. The sample can be glued (use a gentle adhesive or double-sided sticky tape) directly onto the card. If the fabric is semi transparent it may be necessary to place a piece of white paper beneath it to prevent the colour of the card from showing through. Now cut a frame (Fig.20b) from a piece of the same coloured card or the same colour as the background fabric, making the inside dimensions fractionally smaller than the edge of the sample. Place this over the sample to check that it fits then glue it down over the top (Fig.20c) and press firmly in place. The other samples may be arranged in windows round it.

For a special effect, wrap the card frame (Fig. 21) with the same threads as those used on the sample. First paint the corners in the same colours (it is difficult to wrap these) then lay a strip or double sided adhesive all round the frame on the reverse side. Then begin binding the frame firmly and evenly, sticking the beginning and end of each new thread to the adhesive strip and over-wrapping it once or twice to secure it. The last end is secured with a tiny piece of sticky tape.

Round and arched windows look particularly well when wrapped and even more so with an extra (smaller) frame just inside. This is not over lapped by the outer one but is cut to lie edge to edge inside it. The inner one can be wrapped too, or left bare, but if it is wrapped, *be warned* that the thickness of the yarns takes up some room so the inner circle must be a fraction smaller than it would otherwise be.

Fig. 21

←double-sided
adhesive on
wrong side

corners painted

double arched
mount

double
circular
mount

Single Fabric Mount

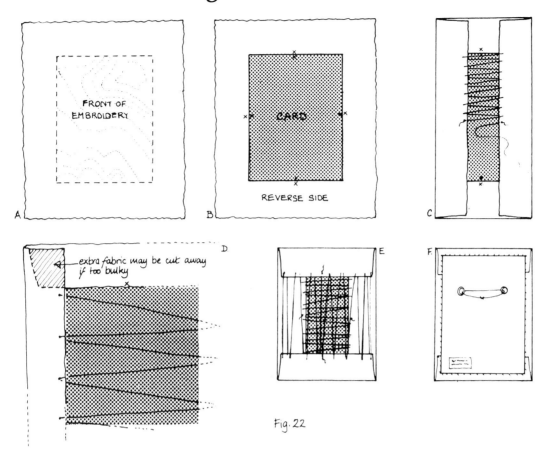

Fig. 22

Embroideries are often worked so that quite a large border of unworked fabric remains all round the design which can be used to enclose a piece of card, hardboard or wood, making a rigid mount ready for a wooden frame. The latter is not essential, merely an option. The following diagrams show how to mount an embroidery in this way (Fig.22).

If the background fabric is fine, loosely-woven or semi-transparent, it will require a layer of more closely-woven fabric, such as plain cotton between it and the card. This will prevent the corners of the card from accidently poking through the fabric mount.

A. Determine the size of the finished embroidery and mark this area with a line of tacking threads.

B. Cut a piece of very stiff card, hardboard or thin wood (or two layers of mounting card offcuts), to fractionally smaller dimensions than the tacked area to allow the edges of the design to fold over the thickness of the card edges. Mark the centre of each side with an x and place these to the same marks on the tacking threads to centralise it.

C. Beginning at the centre of each side, fold two sides of the fabric inwards and hold lightly in place with Sellotape. This is removed when lacing is completed.

Beginning in the centre of each side, as before, and using a strong thread, lace across from side to side towards the top. Secure the thread, then pick up the beginning thread as shown and continue from the centre to the bottom.

D. Fold the remaining two sides inwards, either tucking surplus fabric inside as a neat fold, or, if the fabric is bulky, cutting a square section away as shown.

E. Pin the corners down tightly, lace across in the opposite direction as before, then sew the corners in place with matching sewing cotton and neat, tiny stitches.

F. The back must now be covered with plain fabric (curtain lining is ideal) slightly smaller than the mount. Turn all edges in, neaten corners, pin in place and sew neatly as shown. Fix your personal label to one corner. Rings for hanging can be sewn to the back cover if the frame is not too heavy, and the cord is then threaded through both rings and tied in a circle as shown. Keep the rings well away from the top edge of the frame otherwise they (or the cord) may show when it is hung.

The Worksheet

This takes the form of a large card on which is displayed all the relevant component parts of a project , from the inspirational source (maybe a photograph, doodles or a sketch) through all the design and experimental stages. In other words, the worksheet is like a glamourous sketch-book opened out flat to be seen at a glance or to be inspected more closely. It illustrates the working processes, and progress, of the artist and this helps to make the finished piece more understandable and therefore more attractive. Some worksheets are, of course, no more nor less than an attractive selection of experiments, possibly in one technique, and this makes a perfectly valid display. What one needs to show on a worksheet will depend on various factors, some of these being

a. the requirements of the course tutor and/or assessor,

b. the requirements of a professional artist,

c. to show a technique and its development,

d. to explain working processes to a class, selection committee, a client or prospective employer, and so one must balance the display by including everything which is of interest (particularly visual) and eliminating any parts which are not of the very best personal standard.

What you are left with must now be arranged attractively to produce a unified and artistically coordinated display known as a worksheet.

Here is a checklist of possible items for inclusion:

a. inspirational source of design, if any,

b. working drawings, sketches, explorations in other media

c. developments from these, paper-cutting patterns, borders, motifs

d. colour schemes and inspiration, tonal arrangements, alternative proportions

e. fabrics, threads used, textural experiments, stitches

f. sketches of garments, details, made-up details in fabric

g. sketch or plan of finished product

h. alternative techniques, if any.

It is usually not possible to put all the information about one project on one worksheet; two or three may be needed. When display space is limited, there are alternative methods of presenting this material in a different format and these are discussed further on in the book. This also applies to arrangements of individual pieces and multiple displays.

Textile samples cannot simply be stuck onto display board as they tend to look crumpled and messy, edges uneven and frayed, showing that our thrill at beginning them was often not sustained throughout the hours (days? weeks?) it took us to make them. After all that effort, they must be carefully prepared, matched up with card of a sympathetic colour and given specially-made windows to show them off. The difference this treatment makes to even the most ordinary sample is quite phenomenal, especially when it becomes part of a larger display. Sketches and drawings , paper designs and painted patterns can also be mounted in windows, though some tiny pieces may be glued on if preferred: this is a personal choice and will depend on the purpose of the worksheet.

An Embroiderer's Worksheet

Designing is an important element in the embroidery student's syllabus and this display is intended to show a series of developments based on the lines, tones and colours of a piece of agate and also to add textural effects which will not intrude upon the scheme. Experiments in cut-paper allow the student to move pieces around for a variety of arrangements: experiments in techniques are a way of exploring the use of textures and colours on the lines to see which ones are most effective. The larger sample is required when techniques are combined, though this one may not necessarily be the ultimate result used in the finished project.

Top left: the source of the design may be a photograph or sketch or, in this case, a simplified drawing of a piece of agate.

centre: a coloured pencil exploration to discover the colours seen in the agate photograph.

right: a black and white pen drawing of the tonal values.

Second row, left: a cut-paper design made from a painted sketch to explore the re-arrangement of tones.

centre: wrapped cards showing the threads used in the samples.

right: another cut-paper design with more accent on the negative spaces.

Third row, from the left: samples of blackwork cutwork, stitchery and quilting.

Bottom: a sample of quilting and applique five panels.

Fig. 23

17

A Knitter's / Crocheter's Worksheet (top)

This display illustrates some of the design processes which lie behind the making of a garment. It shows the source of design, samples of fabric, colours and yarns, borders, details and a general plan. These requirements will vary according to the garment, its design and construction and also to the needs of the designer. The arched shape behind the figure echoes the shape of the drawing and also helps to emphasise the architectural theme, as do the cut-paper decorations on the extreme right.

Top left and the two pieces below: photographs of medieval tile patterns.

Centre left: samples of knitted / crocheted units and border patterns which will be used on the garment.

Centre right: pen and coloured pencil sketch of the garment with a flat plan next to it. Below is a display of the yarns made into "butterflies" (see page 29).

Bottom right corner: two covered buttons made to match the coat show alternative colour arrangements.

A Patchworker's Worksheet

A project may be influenced more by a technique than by an outside source of inspiration. In this case, strip patchwork and log-cabin patchwork influence the design of the two bags and though this display is much less complex than the other two, its impact is just as great. There are no working drawings here (these may be shown on another related worksheet), only fabric samples and the two finished bags to show how the fabric design may be used. All the examples are in black, tones of grey, white and silver and re mounted in windows on charcoal grey card.

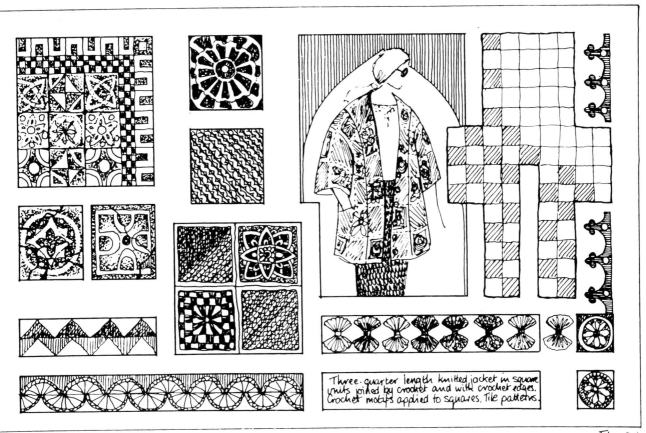

Three-quarter length knitted jacket in square units joined by crochet and with crochet edges. Crochet motifs applied to squares. Tile patterns.

Fig. 24

Fig. 25

Choosing the Format

You may prefer to arrange your samples in a vertical format instead of a horizontal one, or vice versa, and your reasons may be influenced by any of the following:

a. the space available to you for display, i.e. the size of display screens or wall, or even the lack of these facilities:

b. the size and shape of your samples and the number of them:

c. the method of transportation and handling:

d. storage facilities:

e. any other requirements, e.g . postage size, competition specifications .

All these factors should be considered at the outset before you begin measuring and cutting. Sometimes a folding worksheet is preferable (Fig. 26a) when, for instance, wall space is limited. The folding format is particularly useful for teachers who often need a stand-up display during a lecture or for the duration of a workshop. It consists of two worksheets which are joined together like the covers of a book, and this idea can be extended to become a zig-zag format (Fig. 26 b) or a triptych (c). In the latter, the two outer flaps are exactly half the size of the piece in the middle so that the display folds flat without extra overlaps.

There are reasons for and against cutting the windows either before the pieces are assembled or afterwards. Choose whichever you find most convenient, but *remember* that cutting the windows after assembly is quite tricky when there are two or more joined cards to manipulate. If you choose to cut the windows before assembly, mark the position of the tape-line to avoid accidently measuring window-space on this part. Be methodical about this; number the cards in order at top and bottom and *concentrate*. Use a linen tape which is the same colour as your card: the method is the same whichever format you choose, but read further on before you decide.

To assemble the pieces (Fig.26)

1. Lay the two pieces of card, wrong sides up, onto the sticky-tape as shown, leaving a tiny space between them. Press down.

2. Pull the top edge of the tape down onto the cards, and the bottom roll of tape upwards to overlap slightly onto the other edge, then cut.

3. Ease out all the air-bubbles, press firmly an run a thumb nail down the centre. Now measu for the window.

Alternative Joinings

If a matching coloured tape is not availabl consider alternative ways of linking the cards t keep them together. One method is to punch hol (at least three pairs) into the edges of the card an tie twisted, plaited, knitted or crocheted cord through as shown (Fig. 27) leaving enough spac between them for the cards to open and close easil You may find this method more attractive tha using sticky-tape and more convenient to dismar tle and re-arrange.

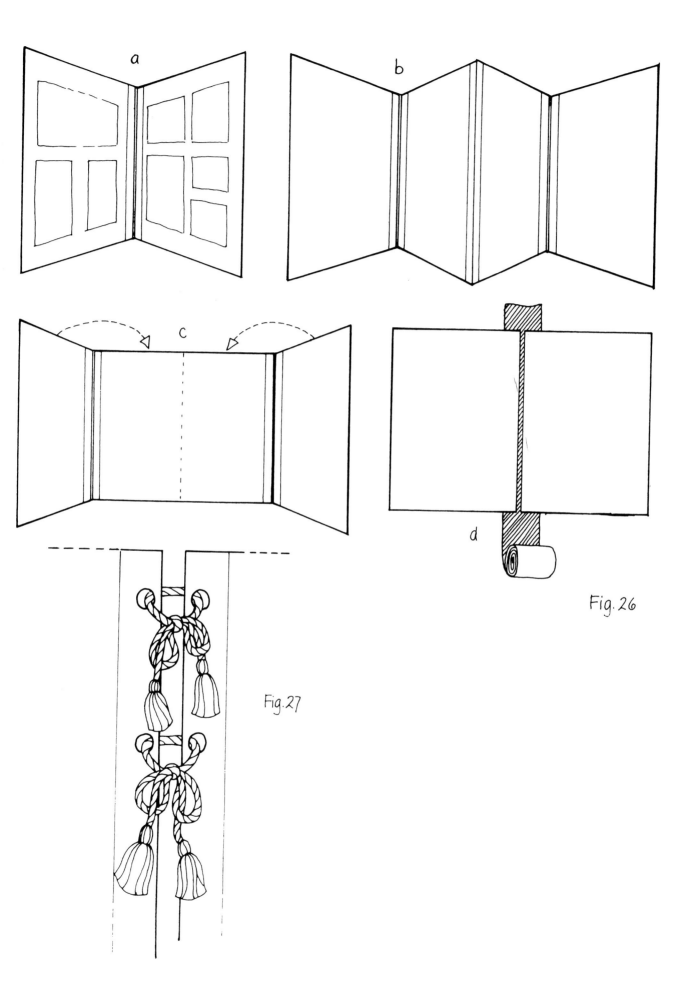

a

b

c

d

Fig. 26

Fig. 27

Mounts with Spines

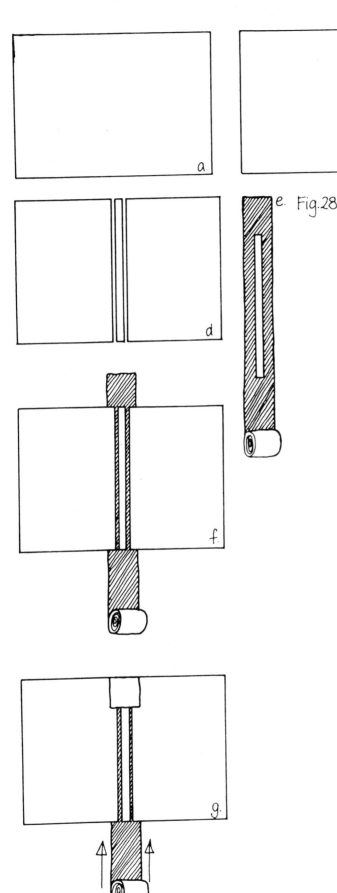

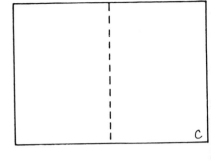

e. Fig.28

If the samples on the fold-over mounts are quite thick, a spine will be needed to allow the cards to lie flat when closed. Take this into account *before* cutting the cards, as the spine is cut from the edge of the card first and the remaining piece is then cut in half, unless you have extra pieces of card (called "offcuts") which can be used for this.

Fig. 28

a. Take one large piece of card

b. Decide how wide the spine must be and cut this from the edge of the card.

c. On the remainder, find the centre, then cut it in half.

d. Place the spine in the centre of the two pieces

e. Leaving the two large pieces in position, remove the spine and lay it along the sticky side of the linen tape. It doesn't matter which way up as it will eventually be covered by the tape.

f. Place the two card pieces at each side of the spine onto the tape, checking that the top and bottom edges are perfectly level. Leave tiny spaces as shown.

g. Pull the tape down over the top edges of the cards as shown, press down firmly, then pull the roll of tape upwards to meet it. Overlap slightly then cut. Press out air-bubbles. Run a thumb-nail down the spaces to press the tape together at back and front. Turn the cards over and smooth the tape on the right side. Now measuring for the window can begin.

Multiple Arrangements

A haphazard arrangement looks slovenly and baffling: aim for an ordered arrangement which will invite closer inspection.

The following points may help you to achieve this:

1. Small pieces are often more effective when grouped together; they create a greater feeling of unity and impact.

2. Balance is more important than symmetry. Try to judge the "weight" of a subject by colour, tone, texture and size. These affect the importance of a piece and determine its position on the worksheet. This, in turn, affects its relationship to the other pieces and the overall balance. The largest piece is *not necessarily* the most important, and the darkest need not necessarily be placed at the bottom. Shuffle the samples round to see the different effects and judge the effect for yourself.

3. Too many samples may mean that you will need to make an extra worksheet; too few may require a smaller worksheet.

4. Trim samples to the required dimensions to make them fit together more easily.

5. Allow generous borders and spaces between samples otherwise the effect becomes too crowded, the card is weakened by too much cutting and extra fabric on the back tends to overlap and cause problems.

6. To create a greater sense of order and standardisation, consider the following suggestions:

a. make all your samples colour-related and mount them on a card of the same colour-family.

White and neutral colours are safe to use as they show up stronger hues to good advantage. Black is useful too, for bright colours but don't regard it as safe for anything. Gold and silver is good for use with metal threads: dark colours make a dramatic impression while pastel-colours co-ordinate well with the same pastel-toned samples to give an impression of all-over softness.

b. Present one technique with related design material.

c. Present one design in a selection of technique experiments.

d. Cut-paper designs, borders, motifs, pattern-making.

e. Fabric-making experiments to show density and drape.

f. Construction techniques in dressmaking.

7. Avoid "staggering" small pieces; they usually look better in a straight line. However, pieces can overlap onto each other when the relationship is very close and you wish one sample to merge into another one deliberately. See Fig.29. This works particularly well with strangely-shaped pieces which will not fit into a standard window.

8. Make the two side-border widths equal (see Fig.30), the top border *either* the same or wider, and the bottom border equal to the top or wider, but *never narrower*.

9. Be aware of the spaces between the windows; they are just as much a part of the design overall as the window-spaces and the samples.

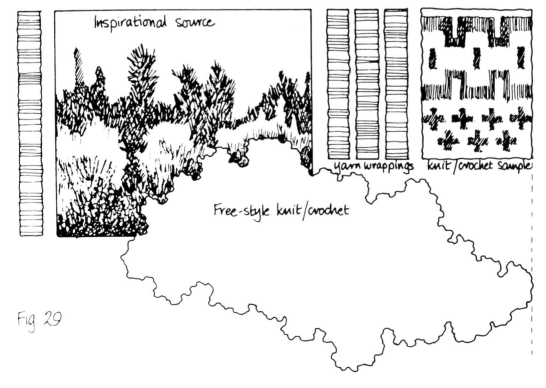

Inspirational source

yarn wrappings   knit/crochet sample

Free-style knit/crochet

Fig 29

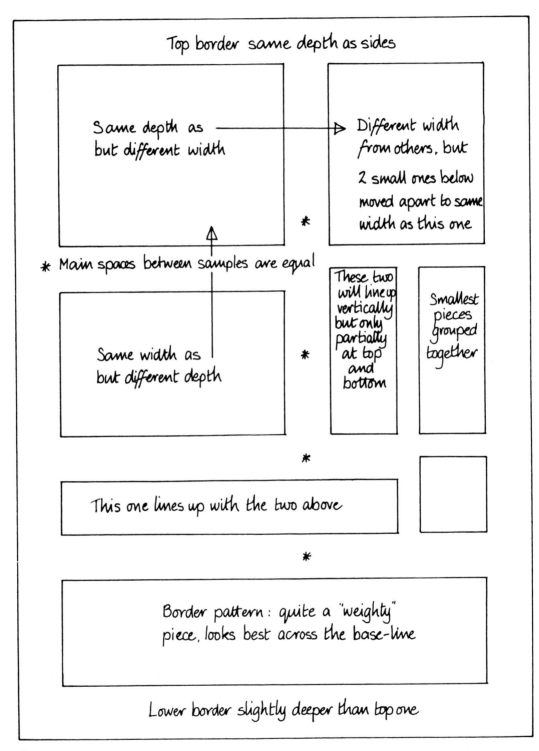

Fig. 30

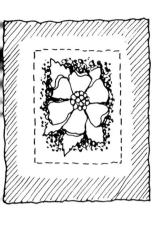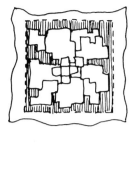

Fig. 31

Fitting several differently-sized samples on one worksheet can usually be made simpler by trimming them so that they have at least one dimension in common. The four samples above (Fig. 31) are all of different sizes, but by careful measuring, borders can be indicated (the dotted lines) which reduces them all to the same width or the same length. The two samples on the left show that, after leaving a narrow border beyond the dotted line, the rest can be trimmed off. The other two samples are too small round the edges to be trimmed. Now they have some common dimensions which make it possible to line them up together.

Two different arrangements (Fig. 32) of exactly the same pieces show that there are many possible ways of achieving good balance. Notice how the smallest windows are grouped together in both arrangements.

Fig. 32

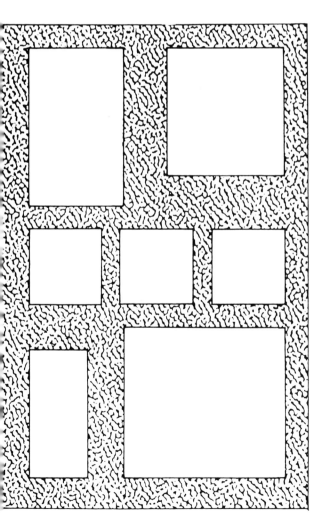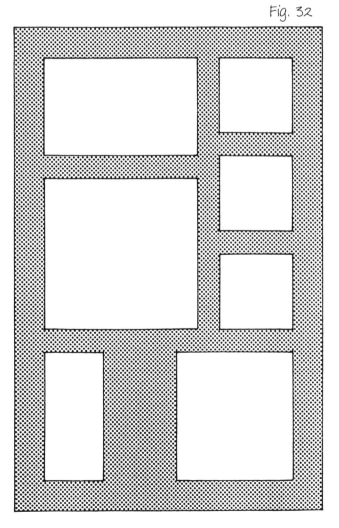

Recording and Measuring

Having decided upon an arrangement which appears balanced in tone and size and allows enough space between samples for them to be glued in place without overlapping behind, the next stage is to plan the windows, record their position and measure. The problem now arises of how to remember where the bits and pieces go when you turn the card over to draw on the back. Some people advocate using a compass-point to mark where the corners come on the opposite side, but I find that this hit-or-miss method does not guarantee that lines and corners will be accurately aligned. If you are using white card (i.e. white on both sides) there is less of a problem. Simply treat the side on which the samples are lying as the reverse side and make all your measurements and notes on that side while the samples are in situ, but remember that *the arrangement on the right side will now be reversed.*

If the samples are arranged on the coloured side, the card must now be turned over so that measurements can be made on the white side. There is a choice of methods for doing this so that a record is kept of where the various bits were, and their spacings. Choose whichever method suits you best.

1. Use a polaroid camera to record where they are. Then, before you remove them, measure each one and make a note of the window size required and write this underneath each sample on the right side. This bit will be cut out so it does not matter about the writing. When you turn the card over you will have a record of the position of each sample and its individual measurement. The space can be worked out from that information.

2. Make a sketch (see Fig. 33) of the layout before you move the samples. On the sketch, make a note of the measurements of each window and the space between. If some samples have the same or similar dimension write on your sketch which bit goes where so that there is no mistake. Keep this sketch in front of you as you measure the windows on the reverse side of the card, remembering to reverse all measurements. For extra re-assurance that you have it the right way round, hold your sketch up to the light and look at it from the reverse side. *This is how you will be measuring and cutting it.* It helps even more if you can re-write the main measurements on the reverse side of the sketch too.

Take time, and concentrate at every stage. Keep the samples handy so that a check can be made on your measurements before you cut. If there are pieces to be glued onto the worksheet without windows, keep these until last and attach them once the other pieces are in position. Follow the mounting instructions as for the single window mount on pages 8 to 10.

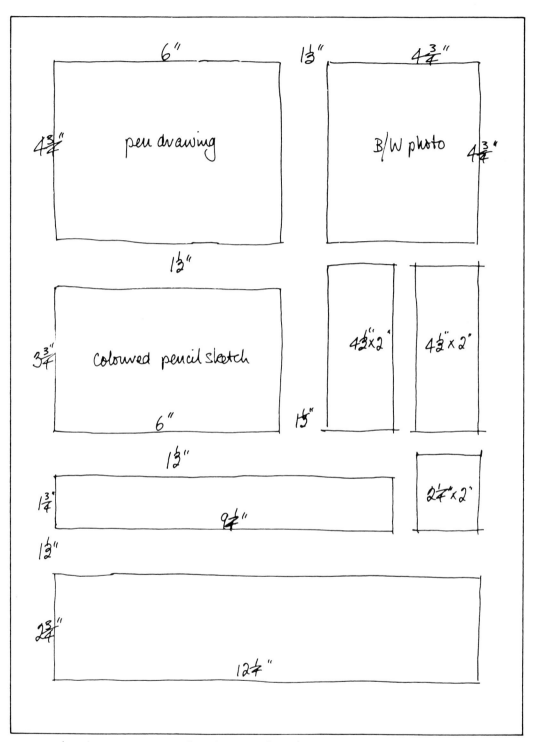

This is the sketch, drawn free-hand while the samples are lying in position on the R.S. of the mounting-board. When the samples are removed, this will be the only record of their position. All measurements are made on the reverse of the board. Hold the sketch up to the light to see how the "cutting side" looks.

Fig. 33

Preparation of Fabric and Threads

It is often necessary to show which materials have been, or will be used in a project and there are several ways of doing this which help to make a worksheet more attractive.

Fig. 34

a. and b. Fabrics are usually cut into rectangles with pinking shears to prevent fraying. To show the nature of the fabric, only the top edges are fastened down so that the rest is loose enough to be touched, though this is more necessary to the dressmaker than, say, the embroiderer. If the tactile quality of the fabric is not so important, it may be worthwhile to back these small pieces with iron-on interfacing to give them extra body. Iron the interfacing onto a small area of the fabric first, *then* cut out the shape. The arrangement of pieces will depend on the area available on the worksheet but, more importantly, it will be dictated by the style and nature of the garment and the fashion drawing. A formal garment calls for formality of presentation; a more casual style suggest a random arrangement. The pieces are often shown, in drawings, to be attached by pins but for longer-term displays there is a danger of rusting and other damage, so I suggest using double-sided sticky tape or a fabric glue. Staples do not look good on a worksheet.

c. Threads and yarns can be wrapped round card strips which have had double-sided sticky tape fixed to the reverse side. Cover the extreme top and bottom edges with yarn, or leave a tiny bit bare and place several strips together inside a window mount. All ends should be stuck to the reverse side and wrapping should be even and close.

d. Small lengths of threads can be displayed as a fringe on card which is the same colour as the worksheet. The one shown here is the actual size required and threads should not be too long in case they interfere with another part of the worksheet. The strip of card is glued onto the mount either horizontally or vertically.

e. The fan-shaped wrapping is an extension of the wrapped strip idea (c) though this is even more decorative and shows off the yarn even more. The card is cut to the shape and size you see here: several of these together will form a complete circle and they can also be arranged to form a border.

f. Butterflies make an attractive yarn display rather like flattened uncut pom-pons. Each side of the bundle is pulled down a little, the end is fastened into the centre and the whole unit is glued to the worksheet. Avoid making them too large; the size seen here is usually adequate.

g. For colour experiments, fine and delicate threads can successfully be wrapped over square cards in both directions to show combinations of colours in the centre portions. It is essential to wrap less closely than the other two methods to allow the underneath colour to show through. Coloured cards also make a difference to the threads which are wrapped round it. Use a piece of double-sided sticky tape on the reverse side to anchor ends of threads.

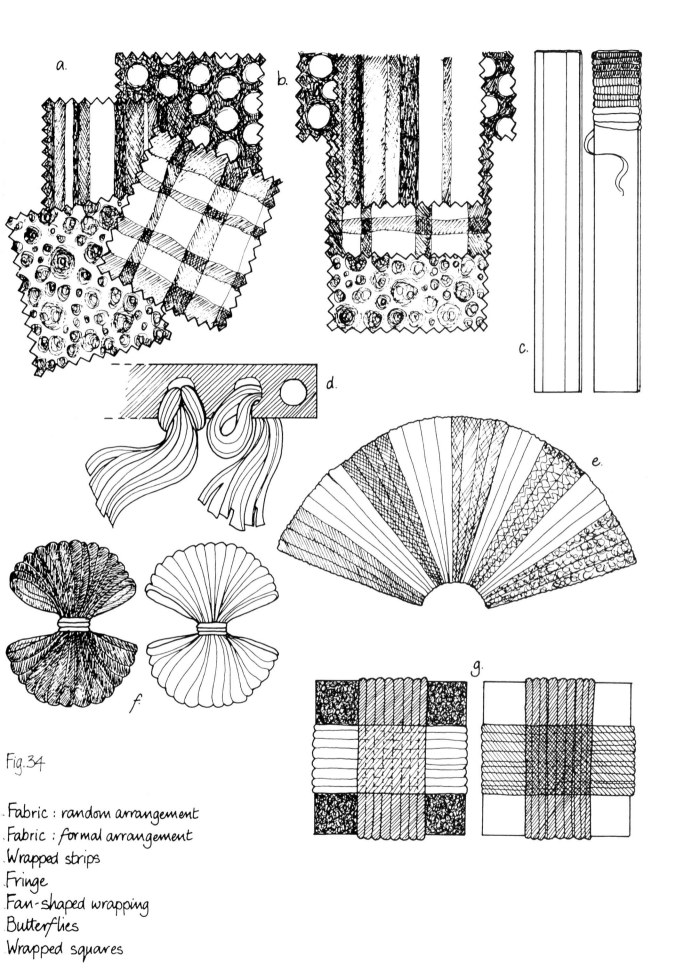

Fig. 34

a. Fabric : random arrangement
b. Fabric : formal arrangement
c. Wrapped strips
d. Fringe
e. Fan-shaped wrapping
f. Butterflies
g. Wrapped squares

Annotations and Lettering

Some textile artists regard annotations on display material as essential, otherwise, they say, how will viewers understand what they are looking at? Others are adamant that notes are out of place. Whatever your view, or the views of your tutor (discover these before you begin), any notes on samples for display should be regarded as part of the layout and therefore must not intrude on the overall design, but complement it.

Notes must, of course, be part of ordinary coursework and these are placed along-side the samples in files and notebooks, but while these are "for your eyes only" to a certain extent, the annotations on the worksheets are part of your public image and should be of the same high standard, in every respect, as the rest of your work.

The following suggestions may help.

1. On a rough note pad, first write your annotations to get a feel of what you need to say, how few words you can use, the construction of the sentence or phrase, spellings, etc.. Don't be "wordy" but try to be concise. Leave out your feelings and the traumas which surrounded the exercise and just write down what it is.

2. Your grammar must be impeccable, even for annotations. If in doubt, get other people to read what you have written to check on this. For instance:

"a. A photo of a garden that I used to sort out colours from for my sample on the right."

This can be said more attractively and concisely as, "a. Inspirational photograph of garden from which colours were selected for sample (b)"

Eleven words instead of nineteen!

3. Spellings, especially names, must be correct. Capital letters must be observed too.

Credits should be given to anyone whose property appears however briefly, in your work. This should always be checked with them first, as someone whose house you used in a photograph may not wish to have it identified for security reasons.

4. If the card is dark-coloured, the writing will have to be done on labels. Your tutor may wish you to make your own labels or you may prefer to use the bought stick-on type which can be written on first before fixing to the worksheet. The size of these should relate to the size of the samples, to your writing or printing (see below), and to the space allowed for them between the windows. Over large labels tend to swamp the display and draw attention away from the more interesting parts.

5. The words may be either
a. Hand written, but only in perfect Italic script.
b. Typewritten; always acceptable and most people's choice.
c. Transfer lettering, attractive but time-consuming and expensive.

The scale of the letters must relate to the size of the label and the words should be centred exactly in the middle. It helps to do this if the words are pencilled in first to see how much room they take up, or practice on your typewriter to see how they fit into the space.

For hand written labels, use a calligraphy pen and black ink or an artist's drawing pen.

Placing of Annotations

Generally speaking, there are two main choices, one is to look for a space in the layout where a block of annotations can be used to level up some of the windows. The other is to give each window or unit on the display a separate label. The following notes refer to the diagrams on the opposite page.(Fig. 35)

1. A block of annotations fills in an awkward gap caused by the different sized samples. It lines up with the top pieces and helps to unify the display, but because it is not clear which note refers to which piece, each one must be labelled (as shown) with an a. b. or c. or with numbers. The letters or numbers are always placed in the same position so that the viewer knows where to look without having to search. In details such as this, consistency is important. A block of annotations is a good way of solving the labelling problem when there are many scattered and odd-shaped bits on the worksheet. Individual labels would probably make it look even more "bitty".

2. With the same layout, an alternative method is to place labels separately like this, but if there is doubt about what they refer to, they should be pin-pointed with the words "above" or "left". The one at the bottom does not need this extra information.

3. Each label occupies the same position in relation to its sample as all the others and is far enough away from its neighbour not to cause confusion to the viewer. This is important, as labels too close to another sample are ambiguous and counter-productive. In this case, no a. b. c. information is needed.

4. A block of annotations in the centre of this display helps to link the totally different sizes above and below. This is a symmetrical presenta-

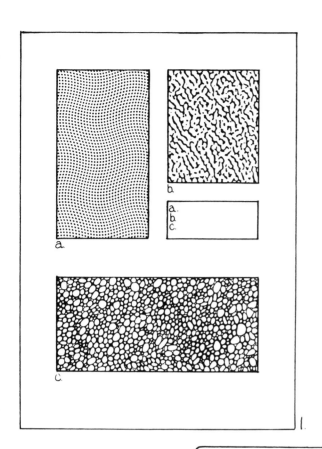

1.

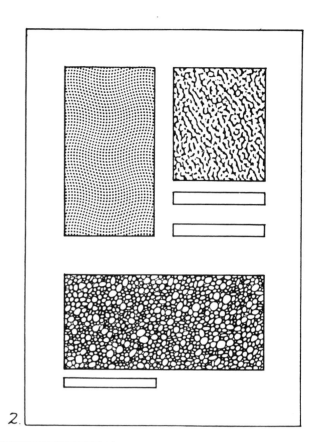

2.

Inspirational photograph of
garden from which colours were
selected for sample

5.

Fig. 35

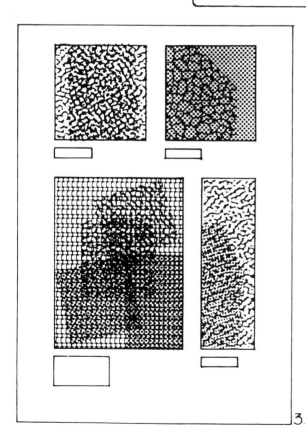

3.

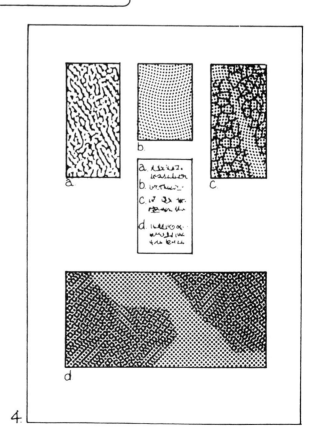

4.

tion and has been given a. b. c. references in the bottom left-hand corners on the mounting-board, not on the samples themselves. If the mounting-board is a dark colour, use white paint and a fine brush.

5. As with small labels, the wording of a composite label, (i.e. for several samples on the same worksheet) must be spaced to fill the whole area. I will help if the words are first roughly written out in a sketch of the label. They can then be spaced more accurately so that the words reach from side to side equally and with no large, uneven or blank spaces left over.

Fig. 36

Decorating your Worksheet

This aspect of worksheet presentation could be regarded as an optional extra (though I know some tutors who insist on it!) but one which is well worth the time and effort. It adds a great deal to the impact of the display and also helps to co-ordinate the various component parts by establishing a common theme, colour and unity. It almost goes without saying that the decoration should be entirely appropriate in scale and style to the textiles on display, and this is something which takes time to discover until one becomes practiced at it.

One way to gain ideas for decoration is to visit other exhibitions of craftwork (particularly examination/ assessment exhibitions) to see how things are done there. Another way is to go window-shopping with the intention of noting the many ways of displaying accessories and other visual material which can be adapted to your own uses. Look also at fashion books by Erté who was particularly brilliant in methods of presenting fashion ideas in a semi-fantastic style. Remember that your display does not have to be too realistic or "down-to-earth" on these occasions; you are trying to "put yourself across" and to show that you have style, flair, creative and artistic ability. Let your ideas out (under control) and keep the down-to-earth image for later during the business negotiations.The observation of current display trends previously mentioned is also an important way of keeping one's own ideas from becoming clichéd and down-right old-fashioned. You cannot afford to subscribe to this image of yourself at this stage.

There are more ideas for decorating worksheets than can be illustrated in one book: for every collection of samples and projects, a different design is possible. There is no chance of running out of ideas. The illustrations here broadly cover various styles and attempt to show how they can enhance the samples alongside.

Which comes first, the sample arrangement or the background design? Strictly speaking, they both come together at the same time, but until you are totally confident about making windows and arranging samples, leave the background design to take care of itself at a later stage. Eventually you will discover that the way you arrange your samples will simultaneously spark off ideas about the background, then you can design both together. Important note: samples are never mounted until the background decoration is clean and dry; this avoids getting paint and glue on the precious bits.

Aims

Try to create a visual connection between the style of the samples and the background decoration. If there is a mixture of styles in your samples, then aim for a main colour, main subject, theme, technique or motif and try to link them together with this. Aim for connections.

Aim for simple, un-cluttered effects. A too-fussy or over-textured background tends to detract from (even camouflage) the items on it. The final question should be, does it make the samples look even more attractive?

Dotting extra bits about "just to fill in the gaps" is not the purpose of the background decoration. All the examples here illustrate how the textile pieces are extended into the whole design. Aim to create unity.

Avoid putting pretty frames around the windows; this is now out-dated and not at all artistic.

Techniques to Try

1. Cut paper shapes; different sizes; coloured or patterned paper picking up the main colours used, scattered at random (with care !) or more formally in a pattern.

2. Stencilling: use cut paper shapes and stipple round them with thick poster paint and an old toothbrush or sponge. Practice first. Again, the colour is significant.

3. Use stippling and marbling techniques, car-paint sprays, glue-and-paint mixes and other messy techniques, whatever is at hand, to produce colour/texture effects as an overall design. This sounds rather frenetic but is really no more time-consuming than other methods, and can be extremely effective, especially where an unspecific kind of decoration is required. Sprinkle gold-sparkle dust onto wet surfaces for extra effect; this looks particularly good with metal-thread work.

4. Use letter shapes on the background, especially if you need to convey a message or repeat letters already used in the design.(See Fig.36)

5. If you have striped pieces amongst your samples, place them on a board of stripes which run in the opposite direction, using the same colours but in different tones (i.e. paler or darker, brighter or more muted). You can do this by pasting strips of plain or patterned wrapping-paper at irregular intervals from top to bottom or from side to side. Don't overdo it!

6. Makers of lace samples, whether bobbin, needle-made, tatting, knitting or crochet, may con-

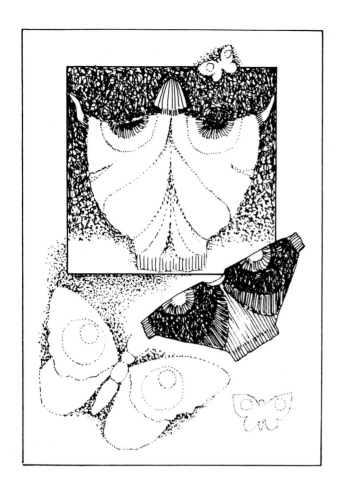

Fig. 37

ider having a huge enlargement photocopy made of one of their pieces (or from a photograph) and fixing this to the board to be used as the overall background to their lace samples. The windows are cut out of this enlargement so that the backgrounds surrounding the samples are plain, usually black. I would not recommend using a colour with this idea, as tradition is so strong in this area where monochrome displays are considered more acceptable. Discuss this with your tutor if in doubt.

7. Motifs from books on art nouveau and art deco make attractive backgrounds and linking-units for small pieces, but only where the style of the samples relates. They look particularly well used with floral and foliage subjects.

Fig .37

Top left

Two samples only, one a fashion-drawing of the back of the garment, the other a knitted piece showing a bat-wing sweater based on the same idea of a butterfly. Two entirely different shapes: the large plain cut-paper butterfly emphasises the theme and the similar shapes, and the two smaller versions add to the swinging motion of the design. They also help to break up the hard edges of the square, making it more compatible with the other more irregular shapes.

Top right

A black and white line design on the background picks up the marbling theme of the subject in the window, which is in colour. In cases where the design flows off the edges of the sample, like this one, (known as "bleeding"),it is always worth considering whether this can be extended in some way onto the background. If the card mount is white, coloured pencils can be used to good effect to produce soft, muted lines and shapes.

Bottom left

Cut paper leaf shapes of plain or gently-patterned paper are used to make a low-key border pattern which helps to emphasise the shapes on the samples. Larger versions have been used on the left, this time as stencilled patterns, though the formal arrangement continues throughout.

Bottom right

Another sample which is capable of overflowing onto its surroundings is this collection of knitted or crocheted cables. Celtic strapwork designs could have been extended precisely at top and bottom, but here the design from Islamic architecture is of a slightly different character. The function of this is not only to extend the design but also to show the visual connection between the two styles

and to accentuate the angular nature of one as opposed to the curvilinear nature of the other. The lines can either be drawn in black ink or painted in the same natural colours as the sample to look like stone-work. Gold paint could be used to high-light the bits above and below the sample: this extra touch aids integration, helping to avoid a too-sharp definition between the two and to focus attention.

Fixing the Worksheet to the Display Board

As far as possible, discover beforehand what the display area facilities are and what the fixing arrangements will be. Then arm yourself with the following materials:

Glass-headed pins, the stronger the better

Macrame T-pins, from craft-supply shops

Drawing pins/thumb-tacks - the heavy-duty variety

Sticky-fixers - square foam adhesive pads

Velcro pads - self-adhesive strips or pads,with a furry surface

Scissors. Sticky-tape, staples and other fixing-devices, except pins, should not be visible when fixing is completed.

Note: if someone else will be fixing your work to the display-board in your absence, it is a good idea to mark the top and bottom of each card *on the back* with the words TOP and BOTTOM to avoid the possibility of something being placed upside down by accident. This can happen quite innocently when other people are not familiar with your work. Needless to say that if you will not be handling your own work, *every single worksheet* should be labelled with your personal details.

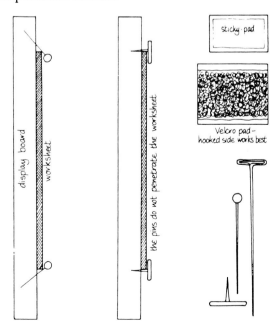

display board

worksheet

the pins do not penetrate the worksheet

sticky pad

Velcro pad –
hooked side works best

Methods

1. Drawing pins/thumb tacks are OK for single card thickness and heavy paper but if your worksheet has now become thicker because of the samples behind it, these will not work. The diagram (Fig.38) shows how the pins are placed below and above the card to support it, NOT THROUGH THE CARD ITSELF. The card rests on the shaft of the pin and the wide head keeps it in position.

2. Glass-headed and T-pins are used when the worksheet is too thick for drawing pins. Here the pins are used to support the card (see the diagram) and are placed at an angle as shown but *not into the card itself*. For a heavy worksheet, three or four may be needed along each side, (i.e.12-14 pins).

3. Sticky-fixers are very strong but are also extremely hard to remove both from the card and the display board. They should be treated with great caution. Always ask before using them.

4. Velcro pads are excellent on fabric-covered display boards and are strong enough to bear heavy cards BUT they lose their effectiveness with age and use, so always carry a new supply with you for replacements. They can be fixed in place on the backs of your worksheets in advance, but take care that they do not come into direct contact with your samples or they will cling to them and may damage them.

Notes, Extra Samples and Reference Material

There is usually much more material in the form of experiments, notes and references amassed during a course which must be kept in an ordered fashion where it can easily be found, and then seen as part of the display. The way in which this material is filed and presented is as much an indication of the student's attitude as are the worksheets and finished projects, so it makes sense to take as much care over this as with the larger pieces. Again, a certain colour co-ordination and unified style brings the display more sharply to the attention than one which is messy and anonymously un-stylish.

A4. Small pieces, cuttings, notes and photographs should be stuck neatly onto A4 paper then slipped into A4 transparent plastic wallets to keep them clean and safe. A separate file (as seen in Fig 39) for each subject is needed so that reference is easy. Label everything clearly while the memory of it is fresh. Scrap books are less convenient than ring-binders as the pages are not inter-changeable nor is there a spine to take the thickness of the samples. The ring-binder allows one to re-arrange things whenever necessary, and insert extra material in the correct place. Smaller sample pieces can be attached by their corners to stiff A4 paper or thin card and filed away like this in plastic wallets which will protect them from dirt and fraying. Alternatively, a box can be used as for the A3 sized cards.

A3. Larger samples and reference material can be presented in a half-box as seen in Fig. 40. This allows them to be seen, used and transported easily and safely and makes a neat display. Large, strong and clean boxes can usually be picked up from shops and should be at least 18″/46cms long to allow for extra space at each side of the cards. Check the box for loose bits, staples, etc., and then line it completely with white paper glued inside. Cover the outside with a decorative or plain paper in a colour which co-ordinates with your display-scheme, allowing the top edges to fold inside by about 3″/8cms. Place your personal label with name and subject in a place where it can easily be seen to identify the contents. Plastic wallets for A3 paper can be bought at art-supply shops, but this is not essential. However, for teachers whose students may handle this material regularly, it is probably worth the expense.

Other more unorthodox sizes are usually acceptable, but check with your tutor first. Transparent gramophone record covers measuring 13″ x $12\frac{1}{2}$″/33 x 32cms can be bought quite cheaply in packs at record shops. They make good, sturdy, square covers but have no holes for ring-binders.

You may prefer to have a half-box which holds your cards vertically instead of horizontally, but check that the base is large enough to prevent the unit, when full of cards, from becoming too top-heavy and falling over.

Paper sizes
A4 - $11\frac{3}{4}$ x $8\frac{1}{4}$ ins / 30 x 21cms
A3 - $16\frac{1}{2}$ x $11\frac{3}{4}$ ins / 42 x 30cms
A2 - $23\frac{1}{2}$ x $16\frac{1}{2}$ ins / 60 x 42cms
A1 - 33 x $23\frac{1}{2}$ ins / 84 x 60cms

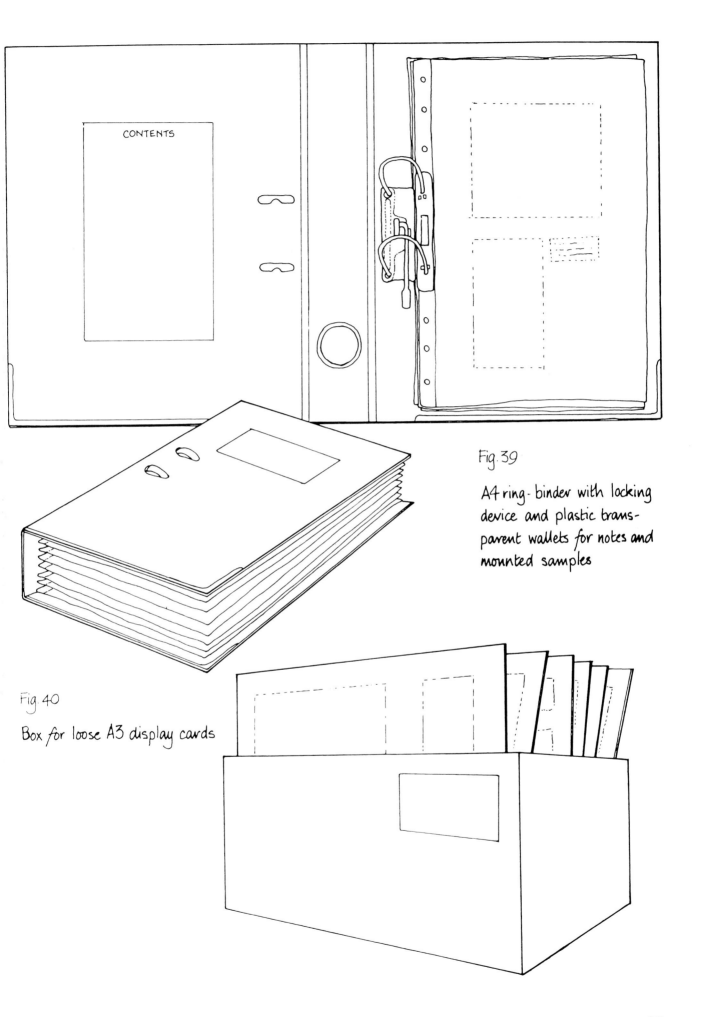

CONTENTS

Fig. 39

A4 ring-binder with locking device and plastic transparent wallets for notes and mounted samples

Fig. 40

Box for loose A3 display cards

Portfolio for A2 papers

Making your own "personalised" portfolio is simple; the advantages are that you can make it to your own specifications, with extra pockets and cover design.

Materials

2 pieces of mounting-card each measuring 32" x 21"/81 x 54cms.

About 8yds of linen carpet-tape 2"/5cms wide.

Measuring and cutting tools as on page 4.

Tapes for tying across the inside and top edges.

Extra decorative papers for covering are optional.

Method

All of the flaps, and one of the 2 sides can be cut from one piece of card as shown in Fig. 41 . The second side is cut from the remaining piece of card,

so there is very little waste.

1. Cut the 5 pieces and arrange them as shown in Fig.42, leaving spaces of 1"/2.5cms between them to accommodate the thickness of the material inside.

2. Lay the card pieces onto 4 strips of tape, sticky side up (shown as dotted lines on the diagram), and fix them in position. Turn the corners down towards you, diagonally, onto the inside.

3. Now lay 4 more strips of tape down onto the first set to cover the sticky gaps between the pieces of card and fold the corners over onto the other side, or cut them off.

4. Make holes in the flaps as shown and tie tape into them. These tie across the inside when the portfolio is carried to keep the contents in position. Extra pockets and bindings can be added as you wish, and a carrying handle too.

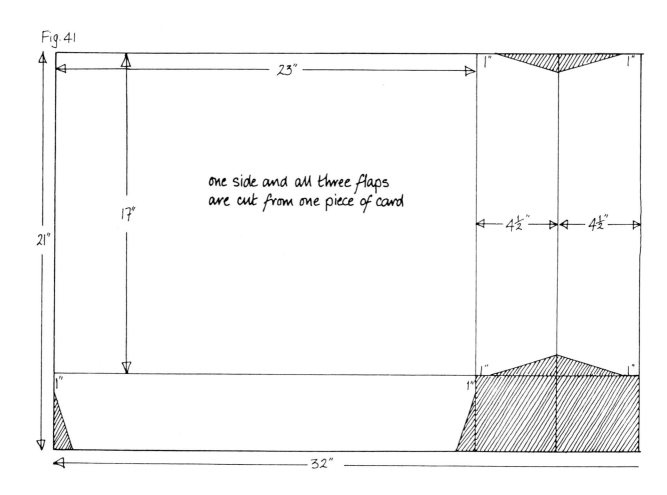

Fig. 41

one side and all three flaps are cut from one piece of card

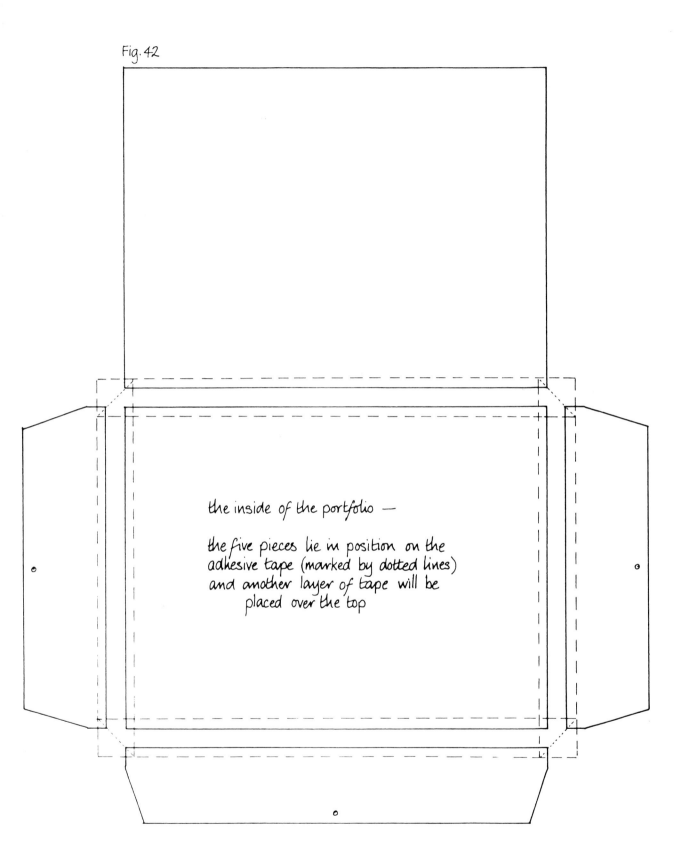

Fig. 42

the inside of the portfolio —

the five pieces lie in position on the
adhesive tape (marked by dotted lines)
and another layer of tape will be
placed over the top

Worksheet Corner-protectors

The constant handling and transporting of worksheets eventually plays havoc with the corners unless you take steps to protect them. These card protectors are simple to make from mounting-board offcuts. Cut out four of the shapes as shown, score along dotted lines, fold up and glue firmly in place. Punch holes in the corners then thread these with strong elastic to link the protectors in pairs. They are placed diagonally as shown, to keep the elastic taut and the corners in position. The thickness of the centre spine can be varied according to your requirements.

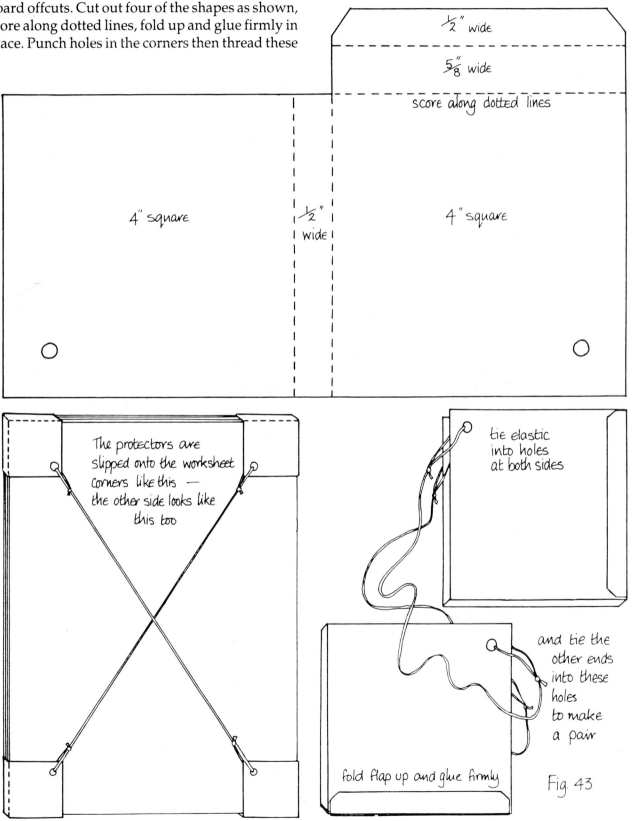

½" wide

⅝" wide

score along dotted lines

4" square

½" wide

4" square

The protectors are slipped onto the worksheet corners like this — the other side looks like this too

tie elastic into holes at both sides

and tie the other ends into these holes to make a pair

fold flap up and glue firmly

Fig. 43